Moths & Flames

K. Kostoń

BookLeaf Publishing

Presentation by *BookLeaf Publishing*

Web: www.bookleafpub.com

E-mail: info@bookleafpub.com

ISBN: 9789357213424

First edition 2023

Her- Blank Slate

The sun does not shine less when people are too warm
It keeps on shining until it feels done
But I only truly shine when I'm completely on my own
Holding back my brightness in front of everyone

Hiding my face on the plane to descend after ten hours
And walk in the setting I've never once been
Basking in the new air and the stranger's bodies
And the way that my face here has never been seen

I throw down my bags in my new empty space
And control my excitement though the dread begins to ring
Staying a year at this college gives a very clear deadline
That I have exactly a year to make me feel worth something

Him- Expectations

I stay surrounded by my books for probably the tenth hour
Staring at the blank essay that I haven't yet typed
As the sky gets darker, my work list gets longer
Adding the responsibility of it being Friday night

When my flatmates comes to tell me that our house is filled again
I'm not surprised that our frat is the most liked
So I follow him downstairs even though I have work to do
And put on a big smile before I'm even in sight

Everybody gives me a cheer when they see my happy grin
And how social I am being since it's Friday
But even though I love them all or at least the few I know
I feel the draining of the battery inside me

I jump around the party and feel close to forgettable

Even though that's not what I've been made to believe
That even though everybody says it wouldn't be the same without me
Nobody notices when I leave

Her- Overwhelmed

The bright lights shine some pink and blue on everybody's faces
The aroma of the cheap beer is so pungent I can taste it
I see bouncing frats in uniform that all look copy pasted
Although it's only half past nine everyone's already wasted

I can see the academia and all the knowledge fading
As all these clever people drink whatever someone gave them
They act civilised through the week and want Friday to come and save them
So all put aside their normal thoughts and decide to act like cavemen

I try to sing along but I'm not sure I know the beat
With all the dancing guys around me someone spills beer on my sleeve
My hands get clammy, and I struggle to stand the body heat

I wonder how I can be the only one, who
suddenly can’t breathe

I barge through the crowd of bodies to finally
step a foot outside
But I am not the only person there, much to my
surprise
He sits on the edge of the patio curled up out of
sight
I assume he’s gonna vomit, until I hear his
gentle cries

Him- Opened

I've never been the most comfortable with my own emotions
So I forcefully swallow them and compress them back inside
When a girl I haven't met yet sits and puts her arm around me
And presents to me her dimples with a warm comforting smile

She rubs her hand against my shoulder and offers me a crowbar
Telling me she can go inside my stomach and help open the crate
The one in which I hide my thoughts and feelings that I'm scared to deal with
She says if I keep on internalizing, my back will crack beneath the weight

Even though this is completely new to me
I throw some puzzles on her lap
She nods along and picks them up
And finds a way for them to match

I learn I need to be more careful
With the thoughts that I express

Because she decluttered my stomach
But left butterflies in my chest

Her- Chill

The words pushed past his lips like vomit
As he spilled out all of his regrets
He told me he always felt the worst
From the pressure of needing to be the best

He did everything others wanted
And his own needs he left neglected
He hated his daily life
But kept doing what was expected

Despite the chilly and heavy thoughts
I look in his eyes and see the fire within
I feel the warmth when his calloused hands
Leave traces of goosebumps upon my skin

He notices the chill I get from his touch
And he looks at me with a face of great concern
He goes inside the house to fetch me his jacket
But despite my waiting, he never returns

Him- Stolen

I wake up the next morning with barely a headache
When I go downstairs, I see the house is still a mess
I am broken hearted but cannot help but wonder
If I would've had a better time drinking like everybody else

There wasn't a way described by letters
To depict the feeling of her skin on mine
Or the way her eyes were so empathetic
And made me feel safe even while crying

Last night I let myself be stolen from her
And took all the drinks my friends put in my throat
Though her image stayed in front of my eyes
And I remained the whole night holding her coat

I told my friends everything I remembered
But didn't have the right words to explain
How despite only spending hours with her
I felt I was in love with a girl with no name

Her- Pupils

I talked on about his pure black eyes
And my friend said her words in time
“Maybe his eyes were just dilated?”
Oh, but not as much as mine

He only shared one part of him with me
Making me feel greedy for wanting more
But the sight of his spine straightening as his chest opened
Was a sight I felt lucky to have absorbed

His feelings he broke off and shared with me
Were stories of which I’d never speak
I cannot tell you them all here
Because they’re all now my secrets to keep

Him- Wrong Body

I can be heavy
But not like that
The weight of my thinking
Only weighs me down

I can be lighter
But that's also bad
Cause the lighter the player
The lighter the stand

The weight of my body doesn't fit with my size
I'm not sure if it's not enough or if I'm too
strong
But whatever the right way
I can tell that mine is wrong

All these thoughts don't bother me
As much as I know they'd bother others
I'd be lighter in my step if all these thoughts
I wouldn't cover

Though it weighs down my lungs and suffocates
me
That I hadn't left enough unsaid
The reason why I can't stop thinking about her
Is cause she's the only one who's ever cared

Her- United States

I feel like a researcher in the Amazon jungle
Watching the birds and where bugs come from
In their unity and their freedom
Being committed to feeling as one

I try to take him off my mind
And sunbathe in the air filled with sweat
As people who drove from different states
Cheer for players they haven't met

I wonder if they feel the pressure he spoke of
When they go to the pitch and play again
Or if their nerves all disappear knowing
That the crowds are here only for them

Maybe I misunderstand the slight nerves
And the feeling is really different
Perhaps the state of anxiety and state of passion
Are really co-existent

The main conclusion of my research
Is that unity is a gift
And that a part of watching football
Is having someone to watch it with

Him- Correct Mindset

Today was the day of the big game
Every time since I met her I woke up the same
Questing if I too packed my boxes
And became a permanent resident in her brain

The waves of people, I stare at stressed
Their screaming cheers reminding us we're best
Wondering if every single body in the crowd
Also has a crate living in their chest

The field is not the place to think of this
I remember what coach Clyde said
That the most important strength to bring
To every game is a good mindset

I felt great with the loss knowing I made a throw
But it was not until we got inside our home
That my fellow players told me I missed
Proving once again, that ignorance is bliss

Her- Unlucky

I was so amazed by the smallest of things
That I didn't question enough details that night
Because if I had paid more attention to the wind
blowing south
I would have noticed that it wasn't quite right

Green grass didn't move the way it usually does
And the leaves didn't fall like they do on normal
days
I was so engulfed by the light in his eyes
I didn't notice that pupils aren't meant to have
flames

I know time does pass, but I guess I forgot
I was too amazed by the way he made it stop
If I only I had questioned the way we both
breathed
I would have realised it was Friday the 13th

Him- Isolated

My beloved brothers and fellow players
Complain about my play in the hall
I'm not sure how they can say it's a group meeting
If I'm only listening through the wall

After talking smack they sit as a team
And all drink beer to wash blame off their tongues
I sit in my room and hear some chatter
There's talk of coming to check on me, but nobody does

I sigh and sit on my bed
I know they have no malicious intent
They know if I pulled myself down from the dumps
I can do it myself once again

Her- Picture Frame

I buy myself flowers from the local lady
And take myself out on a date
If I'm alone on Saturday afternoon
Then that was decided by fate

I explore new buildings I've never stepped foot in
I find pictures of the college football teams
I glance at their faces and wonder if they're friends
And what their bond really means

They all look so different but they all smile bright
Varsity jackets on all of these guys
I don't take much notice of who I see
But one blonde one catches my eye

I rush out my phone and snap a picture
I feel my heart begin to race
His picture looked equally happy to see me
A mirroring smile forced itself on my face

I stare at the picture and look at his clothes
Gasping at the Greek letters I find

I can’t read them but the sign of a frat
Tells me he exists outside of my mind

Him- Exhausted

I've heard it all before
That you have to wait it out
That once you just get out of high school
You'll learn what life's about

I've been told that it gets better
When I most wanted to die
But after 20 years of living
I've decided that's a lie

My first high school counsellor
Told me that pain will never end
And if you want to feel much better
You're gonna have to just pretend

But being a professional actor
Really gets in the way
It gets tiring to walk on eggshells
To not ruin anyone's day

I'm tired of no one noticing
Whether I'm present or if I'm there
If I'm breathing freely or holding my breath
So that others can have my air

I’m tired of forgiving others
When I’m aching at the feet
From avoiding stepping on any toes
And standing so others can have a seat

My most loyal thought I’ve had for years
Is unsurprisingly, really dark
But maybe dying and hurting others
Is the only way for me to leave a mark

These thoughts stay with me in the cold
Parts of my heart where it’s frosty
I pack my bag and get my shoes realising
I’m not tired, I’m exhausted

Her- Invited

Not knowing my odds or whether they're slim
I run to the buildings I remember entering
I stand at the porch with my phone unlocked
And pound at the door so they can hear my
knock

Whoever opens is shown the picture
But most of them struggle to think of a name
They tell me the house he may be in
And inform me he was there at today's football
game

I hold onto my hope and chances
Visiting all houses I get sent to and from
But I cross off home after home
Until I stand at the very last one

A handsome man opens the door
And he greets me with a smile
There is no hesitation in his voice
He tells me I'm searching for Kyle

My blood vessels almost burst
But I try to still look content

He tells me that although my love lives here
Nobody quite knows where he went

He puts his hand on my shoulder
When he sees that my sad spine curved
He tells me there's a party in the evening
That Kyle wouldn't miss for the world

I try to tame myself
And not show that I'm excited
But this is the first time I'm not a plus one
This is the first time I'm invited

Him- Swimming

I do everything you're supposed to do
And go for a walk to clear my mind
I walk past the river that is close to a flood
And wonder what inner peace I'm expecting to find

Accidental thinking fills my eyes with unwanted tears
There's no motivation for the action; I won't be happy with the result
I can spend my whole life pretending I have pride
But deep down inside I know my cup will never be full

This is the only time in my life
That I hope to lose faith in my limbs
After my whole life of forcing myself to succeed
I'm hoping I fail to swim

Her- Saturday

The Southern smell of beer doesn't bother me
anymore
Nor do the bouncing frats spilling drinks all on
the floor
In fact the empty minded happiness is becoming
quite infectious
Maybe the child-like joy in life is something that
could connect us

It had only been 20 hours since I last stood in
this house
Scared to show my face I almost had to give in
to my doubts
But by going a party where I just felt out of
place
I met somebody who's impact nobody could
have replaced

I bump around the party like a pinball with no
drink
I glance around the room remembering his hair
to be distinct
With every passing moment more people come
and start jumping way too quick

The music ringing in my ears makes it
impossible to think

The room becomes too filled
The crowd gets impossible to pass through it
I throw myself outside for air
Only to see someone beat me to it

Him- Sunlight

I know better than anybody
That grief never just recovers
This is the reason I could not have jumped
I'm not good at hurting others

Though the night stayed dark I sat and hoped
That my mood would not worsen
I looked up and saw what I can only describe
To be sunlight as a person

Her arms open wide as she stands in front of me
I open mine back to catch her in her front fall
The tightness of her hug presses on my lungs
But does not resemble drowning at all

Her- Him

He wraps his arms around me on his lap so tightly
As if he's fearful that I will run away
To be truthful the reason I stay on his lap might be
Cause I'm not sure whether this time he'll stay

I cup his cheek and look in his eyes
And hope to absorb all his pain
He unloads his struggles since we talked last night
He thinks he's sounding insane

I part my lips to spill my knowledge
And he listens to my voice
I tell him the good thing about a bad day
Is that it only happens once

Him- Her

She looks stuck for words but speaks
nevertheless
To tell me that she watched my game
I can't help but interrupt with a thumb on her
lips
To finally ask for her name

To tell you the truth, I shouldn't be a fan
I never understood names that were words
But Asia must be the most angelic one
I think I have ever heard

It feels unbelievable to have her in my arms
And at last know her name
To think that even the thought of her
Helped me survive two extra days

Our conversations become much more calm
As we just enjoy each other's presence
She asks me what animal I feel most like
But her blue eyes are luminescent

I feel drunk and mazed in her vivid eyes
That it's hard to think and listen

All I know is the brightness that she brings
Is the light my life was missing

Even in the coldest Autumn nights
Holding her keeps me campfire warm
The lantern that she must hold in her chest
Is different to my internal storm

I look in her eyes and try to squint
Even though for words I became lost
She brightens my face with her wide shining smile
And I tell her I feel like a moth

You

Remember when you feel like you don't do
enough:
Your comfort still warms, and your smile still
shines
Although you walk on earth in only one body
You live in millions of minds.

www.ingramcontent.com/pod-product-compliance
Lightning Source LLC
Chambersburg PA
CBHW051758130826
49812CB00033B/1194
9789357213424